D0897232

Humpty Dumpty:
After the Fall

Introducing the
GO FIGURE KIDS

Paul R. Lamb

BALBOA.
PRESS

A DIVISION OF HAY HOUSE

Balboa Press books may be ordered through booksellers or by contacting:

Balboa Press
A Division of Hay House
1663 Liberty Drive
Bloomington, IN 47403
www.balboapress.com
1 (877) 407-4847

Because of the dynamic nature of the Internet, any web addresses or links contained in this book may have changed since publication and may no longer be valid. The views expressed in this work are solely those of the author and do not necessarily reflect the views of the publisher, and the publisher hereby disclaims any responsibility for them.

The author of this book does not dispense medical advice or prescribe the use of any technique as a form of treatment for physical, emotional, or medical problems without the advice of a physician, either directly or indirectly. The intent of the author is only to offer information of a general nature to help you in your quest for emotional and spiritual well-being. In the event you use any of the information in this book for yourself, which is your constitutional right, the author and the publisher assume no responsibility for your actions.

Any people depicted in stock imagery provided by Thinkstock are models, and such images are being used for illustrative purposes only. Certain stock imagery © Thinkstock.

Printed in the United States of America.

ISBN: 978-1-4525-2149-7 (sc)
ISBN: 978-1-4525-2151-0 (hc)
ISBN: 978-1-4525-2150-3 (e)

Library of Congress Control Number: 2014915586

Balboa Press rev. date: 11/03/2014

GO FIGURE ...

Part I

The Great Fall

Humpty Dumpty sat on a wall;
Humpty Dumpty had a great fall.
All the king's horses and all the
king's men
couldn't put Humpty
back together again.

The Go Figure Kids
Back: Dragon
Lt – Rt.: Francis Lake, Paladin Frizban., Sarah Dippity,
Angus Daye, Chris Elise Knight, Carl "Quackers" Young

Hairline fractures ...

"Oh, boy," said Humpty. "Wouldn't you know it. "Just when I'm supposed to do something worthwhile and important, this happens. I'll never get back together. Why does this always happen to me?!?!!" Grumbling aloud Humpty Dumpty looked up and saw a bunch of kids gazing down at him.

"Looks like you had a great fall, sir," said Sarah Dippity.

"Where are all the king's horses and all the king's men?" Humpty Dumpty returned to Sarah Dippity, looking at the kid next to her.

"That's Quackers," said Sarah Dippity.

Quackers said to Sarah Dippity, "Everyone *is* like Humpty Dumpty."

"Everyone is like me?" Humpty heard Quackers.

Quackers looked at Humpty Dumpty. "Yup, everyone, Humpty! Everyone sits on the wall – their wall of choice. Everyone has a part of them that is riddled already with hairline fractures – perhaps just a small corner of the brain, but there, none-the-less. Hairline fractures belong to all -- to make everyone a whole person. Or, at least, a good egg," said Quackers with half a grin.

crack ... crack ... crack ....

Dragon chirped in, "Yah, I know. For a long time I was denying or totally unaware of the hairline fractures I had. That simply enabled my fractures to become weaker; give rise to even more hairlines. One fracture can propagate another ..."

... crack ... crack ... crack ....

"Is that why you, I mean, all the dinosaurs disappeared?" asked Humpty Dumpty.

"I know they talk of many reasons for our extinction. This one, though, sounds good to me. It could be the extinction of many who do not attend to their hairline fractures," predicted Dragon.

Humpty Dumpty looked at Dragon and said curiously with lengthy wondering pauses, "You are a dragon and you ... and you .... are ... talking ...."

Dragon looked at Humpty and said, "That's nothing. You're an egg ..."

Chris said, "When hairline fractures are unattended the whole person crumbles into scattered pieces like you did Humpty Dumpty."

Angus added, "And rather than 'all the king's horses and all the king's men', only **you**, Humpty, can put yourself back together again.

"Harumph!" said Humpty. "But I'm the Royal Egg!" Humpty said with flair. "So things will happen for me."

"He was such a kind and gentle man…"

Paladin and Frances listened then Paladin added, "When an individual has 'a melt down' or 'flies off the handle', we often hear that this person, is described in the media by neighbours, as 'a kind and gentle person'. More like it, they become a Mr. Hyde! Hyde who is another who avoided attending the hairline fractures. The whole person crumbled, lost control, and behaved in an unrecognizable and shattering manner -- disgusting."

"You're not kidding, Paladin," said Quackers who flirted his eye brows up and down and wiggled his fingers as if playing a flute like Groucho Marx, "crowds gathered and, as a constant topic of conversation, they discussed Hyde with disgust."

All the Go Figure Kids looked at Quackers imitating Groucho and then looked at each other with a pregnant pause of silence followed with a consensual groan. Only Frances Lake laughed ... kind of...

Quackers said, "Ignoring your hairline fractures is the thin edge of the wedge being driven into the fractures. As time passes and more challenges happen in your life the wedge is driven deeper and deeper.

Until ..."

"... IT happens!

What the event will be is unknown –
it seems to 'just happen'! None-the-
less, the wedge is driven in as each
small and inconspicuous challenge
occurs. The event need not be
something catastrophic. In fact,
more often, it is a small, seemingly
unobtrusive incident – but it's
the last straw! You are unaware
of the accumulating effects."
Sarah Dippity finished Quackers'
thought.

Chris said, "I'll tell you a story,
Humpty. A story of two frogs."

The short story of the frogs

Once upon a time there were two curious frogs. One curious frog jumped into a pot filled with boiling water! "OW! This is very hot!!!!" said the frog. And the frog jumped out immediately!

The other curious frog jumped into a pot filled with room temperature water and lingered. "AHHH...' said the frog.

The heat was turned up, though very gradually ... and up ... and up ... and up ... to a boil! The frog paid no attention to this insipid rise in temperature. The frog boiled to death. It croaked! ...

The wreckage ...

"Like the second frog that croaked, the wedge is driven into your hairline fractures insipidly – almost insidiously. You are unaware of it – you crack.

The hairline fractures have grown longer; increased in number; coalesced; and the wedge is driven in one more time!!!!

And then ...

The great fall!

Angus said with a very sinister voice, "You shatter and in some cases – wreckage!".

You ...

"All the King's horses and all the King's men cannot put you back together again, Humpty," said Quackers.

"Yes, consequences happen; different institutions may be involved. Professionals may be called in; medications may be prescribed; and, so begins the attempt to 'put you back together again'.

In the end, though, with all that help, *you* are still the only one who can put you back together again." Humpty didn't see who said that.

It's all about you ...

"Yah, like Humpty Dumpty," said Humpty Dumpty, referring to himself, "they have a great fall! Of course I'd point to myself if I could ... but ... I can't - Had a great fall, yah know." Humpty finished, trailing off.

Sarah Dippity said, "Fortunately, these acts of devastation are quelled by most. Usually, others do their Humpty Dumpty act, yet catch themselves *before* their **great** fall – destructive devastation."

Quackers said, "However, less than the destructive devastation, not tending to your hairline fractures, you can act in a way that is not really you. You're overwhelmed, not yourself. Your hairline fractures are breaking as you have avoided tending them and you cannot hold yourself together..."

Tending ...

"So if I tended to myself, my hairline fractures, every day, they would be fewer and I would be stronger so I wouldn't have a great fall, like I just did," said Humpty.

"That's right, Humpty," said Angus.

"Is it time?" Angus looked at his friends, The GO Figure Kids, with anticipation. "Is it time?"

"Time for what?" Quizzed Humpty Dumpty. "Is it time for you kids to put me back together again?"

"Well, the first step to being put back together," said Chris, "is for you to say '**YES**' to yourself, welcoming you getting back together. Secondly to accept help and say '**YES**' to that help."

"Your life has changed, Humpty. I'm not intending to push 'all the kings horses and all the kings men' to the back of the line, yet, are you ready to work with us, Humpty?

Quackers saw almost an imperceptible affirmation in Humpty's eyes and face and said, "It's time! It's time for the magic question."

"Magic?" said Humpty Dumpty with excitement. "There is a magician to put me back together?"

"We're no circus act," said Quackers. It's magic, though, to perform your transformation. And you, Humpty, are the magician."

"Me?" Humpty Dumpty was skeptical.

"Humpty," Dragon said, "On a scale of 10-1, to put yourself back together again - your transformation - where 10 is the most and 1 is the opposite where do you put yourself on that scale?"

"Make that a big 12," said Humpty Dumpty. Humpty then felt an early stir in his yolk of success ...

"I think we should tell Mr. Dumpty who we are before he does the work," said Frances. "Better the Go Figure Kids you know than the one's you don't know." The other kids agreed.

"Hi, Mr. Dumpty. I'm Frances Lake, Dr. Young's assistant," as she nodded at Quackers. "My pleasure to be here."

"I am Quackers – Dr. Carl 'Quackers' Young. Most call me Quackers. It's my pleasure to know you, Humpty Dumpty. "I'll now hand the baton over to ..."

Hello, Humpty, can I call you that? I'm Sarah Dippity."

"I'm Paladin Frizban, and you can call me Pal -- Nice to meet you, Humpty. I've heard about you, now, for a long, long, long time.

Not as long as Drag, but you're laminated in the history books, Humpty!"

The baton passed around.

"I'm Angus Daye."

"I'm Chris Knight."

"Hi, Humpty Dumpty, I am Dragon," growling at Paladin, "Unlike Paladin, please don't call me Drag. You won't fry but I sure will! I might make you extinct!

"Well, lets start with the end in mind," Quackers said. "When you feel you no longer need us kids what will you be doing?"

Humpty said, "Together again. I'll be doing together again."

"Together again?"

"Yah. Together again."

"What else?"

Yah. Together again and with the skill to keep on tending to myself."

Frances Lake said, "If all you have is a hammer everything looks like a nail. There is a better chance of success with more than one way to accomplish things -- as they are respectful, genuine and valuable."

Sarah Dippity continued, "So let's explain these seven steps or tools to invite Humpty Dumpty to apply and put himself back together again."

Part II

Putting Humpty Back Together Again

Step One

<u>CHANGE YOUR MIND...</u>

Quackers began. "Step one, Change Your Mind. Change your mind is counter-intuitive. It is the easiest AND the most difficult.

"You can change your mind instantly! It's actually possible! You will change *instantly*!

You can have high self-esteem, high confidence, great self-value and worth -- and still be humble -- *immediately*!

Sound miraculous, Humpty? Well, it's not ... It's just hard! Hard to believe!

The rub is that you make it hard for yourself -- because you don't believe in yourself," said Quackers emphatically.

Self-efficacy ...

Quackers glanced at his friends as he kept talking. "You change your mind more than you change your socks. However, it is easier to change your socks than change your mind, when changing your mind involves self-esteem! – your abilities and willingness to put yourself back together again. You have to believe in yourself that you can do it. It's called self-efficacy.

You, Humpty, or anyone else may not consider yourself *worthy* of being put back together." Quackers paused for a moment.

"If you think you're worth a dollar and a half nobody will raise your price.

'Besides, there would be no great loss to the world if you were not back together.' Is that what you think?" Asked Quackers.

'Catch 22' ...

"The thing is you probably DO think you're worth a dollar and a half. How do you change your mind about yourself, your abilities and your value? It's tough! It's a 'catch 22', as in the Joseph Heller book – Catch 22. It's easy to see it as a no win. How do you believe in yourself when you don't believe in yourself? How do you have value when you believe you have no value?"

Believing that you are nothing ...

you *are* nothing.

Stop It ...

If you *do* think that –

STOP IT!

The only one your
judgments must pass
Is the one looking back
in the glass ...

The reality is you are *not* nothing!

You are something!

Your resiliency tank may be close to empty for now, or has it run on empty for a long time? ... This is about filling it up and reclaiming yourself!!!"

Step Two

<u>ACT AS IF...</u>

Quackers continued, **"The real you** is someone with confidence, self-esteem and self-worth.

They are all in you, 100%

And you may not believe that.

So when you don't believe you have any of these core values, then, you must –

Act as if ...

Act as if you have high value or self-esteem!

Act as if you have abilities!

'Play pretend' you believe in yourself!

'Act as if' by imagining you have value, even though you really do!"

Sarah Dippity took over, "Yah, Humpty. "See yourself 'walking tall', or show your value to others without showing arrogance.

Imagine other people appreciating you for you, who you are and what you've done.

Imagine yourself standing on a stage and hearing applause for you!

(Or do you believe you have a better chance winning the lottery. *Or, do you believe you don't even* deserve *to win the lottery so why even bother imagining that!?!?)*"

**If you believe
You will receive!!!**

The give away ...

"Act as if you have value by giving someone else your value.

Your value gets bigger the more you give away.

You may want to help somebody else, even in a simple way.

A nickel's worth of help can
be a priceless resolve! ...

Feed someone who cannot feed themselves; pick something up for someone that they dropped; teach someone how to read; volunteer. Even as *simple* as you deem it, anything will do that helps others.

And stop thinking—'oh, they don't want my help' or some such thoughts. Well, *yes*, they do want your help! If you don't help, who will? -- well ... maybe someone else just might help ... -- but go for it yourself! <u>You</u> help!!!"

Dragon added, "If the other person says 'thank you' or gives you a compliment, accept it and say, whatever fits for the response -- "my pleasure" or 'thank you'."

"Stop minimizing it by saying –

'It's nothing...'
'No problem...'
'This old thing?' ...

When you minimize the other's 'thank you' or compliment, you –

- minimize the compliment,
- minimize the other person and
- minimize yourself.

Simply say **'Thank you!'**..."

Be frank ...

Frances Lake said, "Dr. Young has told me that an example of 'acting as if' is Frank William Abagnale, Jr. This is the man on whom the movie with Leonardo DiCaprio and Tom Hanks, <u>Catch Me if You Can</u>, is based. He acted as if by being a con artist, an escape artist, an impersonator. I'm giving no judgment to his behaviour, here. He is simply an example of 'acting as if'...

You 'act as if' you are someone.

Success ...

Others believed Frank Abagnale. Others will believe you.

Frank believed in himself. You have to believe in yourself.

Eventually the law caught him up. But Frank Abagnale Jr. believed in himself and that's why he was successful acting as if!"

Escape ...

- Impersonate the valuable you! ... even though you are actually valuable!!!
- Con yourself into believing you have high self-esteem! ... even though you actually do have high self-esteem waiting to be set free! ...
- Escape from the shackles of the dark side! ...

Escape your own shackles ...

and believe in yourself!

Believe the Beginning ...
Begin the Believing ...

Step Three

WHAT YOU THINK ABOUT
YOU ACT OUT ...

Quackers shared, "It has been attributed to many, it's been said," --

Watch your thoughts; they become words.
Watch your words; they become actions.
Watch your actions; they become habits.
Watch your habits; they become character.
Watch your character, it becomes your destiny.

The blank mind ...

The language you use in your head is crucial. You talk to yourself all the time - waking or sleeping. And when you think your mind is blank, you're talking to yourself!

So, what do you say to yourself?

Do you tear yourself down, minimize yourself? Or do you build yourself up, tap into and emerge your empowerment?"

Magic ...

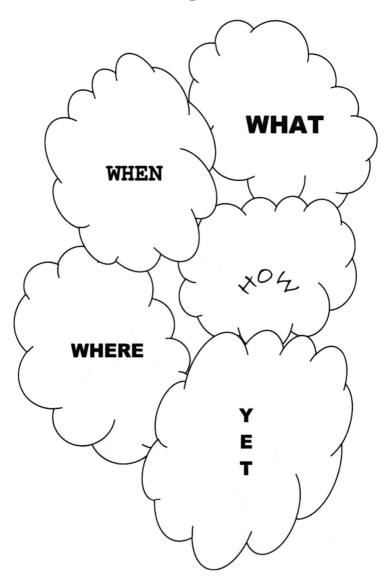

Try me ...

Quackers carried on, "Rather than the word 'why' use the other W's - What, Where, When and the H word -- How.

- ◆ 'Why me?' ask 'How can I try me?'
- ◆ 'I'll never be able to do that.' ask 'when will I do that?' – avoid the answer – *'when the stars fall from heaven'!*

Simply ask yourself the question and your mind will eventually answer you!"

Dragon said, "Replace your words to presume you are accomplished.

Put an optimistic spin on your thoughts and your language ...

Replace –

- 'if' with 'when'
- 'might' with 'will'
- 'this doesn't work', with 'what works?'

Use the word 'yet' in your statement or thought that you have not *yet* accomplished

'I haven't done that, yet.'

Turn your negative thoughts into accomplishing thoughts – rather than 'This isn't working' say -- 'what can I do to make this work'.

You don't *have* a nice day -- you <u>*make*</u> it a nice day."

Rather than 'wait and see',
'act and create'.

Quackers talked of one of his idiosyncrasies. "Take the word 'but' out of circulation -- the word 'but' leads to excuses and rationalizations that have no energy –

'I have confidence _but_ ...'

I can do that _but_ ...'

I did a great job _but_ ...!

And ...

The word 'but' also subverts any compliment or strength you have, or good you've done – 'I did a good job fixing my bike _but_ the rear wheel still wobbles.' – implying you didn't do a good job on your bike.

Substitute the word _'and'_ for 'but'.

'I did a good job fixing my bike _and_ I have to fix the rear wheel, yet.' (Note the word 'yet' presumes you will fix the wheel.)"

Step Four

AFFIRMATIONS ...

"Use affirmations – short positive statements about you. The more senses you use with affirmations the more successful they are.

Making sense ...

Senses

- ◆ Seeing
- ◆ Hearing
- ◆ Tasting
- ◆ Smelling
- ◆ Touching

58

- *Look in the mirror or glass. See* your reflection saying the affirmation ...
- Say it aloud and *hear* yourself
- *Breathe* in deeply before you say the affirmation as if you are smelling the sweet smell of success – your affirmation
- Write them down and, as if in Braille, slowly run your fingers over the words with meaning...

Delicious ...

- Put a simple familiar tune to them to encourage memory ...
- Put them on sticky notes and paste them in conspicuous places for you to see your qualities and value whenever -- like on your mirror, your bedside night table or kitchen cabinets
- Taste the delicious chocolate coated affirmation lingering in your wisdom"

Dragons ...

"Not really talking of me," Dragon said with tongue in cheek, "affirmations question your dragons (dragons live in your unconscious and niggle your conscious).

Your affirmations support your unconscious guide and will chip away at your dragons and self-doubts, like mining for gold until you hit your richness within."

"Write affirmations like this:

Synergy ...

Be specific: You may want to focus on something specific such as your health, self-esteem, your job, love, abundance or weight. The areas of affirmation are endless. It's up to you. If you don't really know what to focus on then focus on your self-esteem, confidence or self-control...

I am ...

- **I** -- Start with the first person -- 'I' - that would be you! ...
- **Present Tense** -- Use the present tense. 'I am...' or 'I have'... or 'I do'...
- **Positive** -- Put a positive spin on it. Say what you want or what you have rather than what you don't want or who or what you are not.

64

Affirmations

◆ I am confident.
◆ I am tall within.

Bridging gives –

◆ I am confident and tall within.
  o A simple tune might be to London Bridge"

Quackers attempted to sing.

"Remember London Bridge? ...

> London Bridge is falling
> down,
> Falling down, falling down.
> London Bridge is falling
> down,
> My fair lady.
>
> I am confident and tall
> within,
> Tall within, tall within.
> I am confident and tall
> within,
> Yes, I am (a-am)."

Response-able ...

- I have value.
- I have courage.
- I take responsible risks.
- I am recreating who I am.
- I am slim and toned.
- I make my job fulfilling.
  - o *(Note: your job doesn't do it, you make it fulfilling.)*

Make it so ...

- I make it a great day.
  (You don't <u>have</u> a nice day, you <u>make</u> your day great.)

- I am in control of myself.
  (You can't control everything but you can control yourself -- your thoughts, emotions and actions – always – all the time.)

Less power ...

Sample affirmations that have less power or energy:

> I *will be* confident and tall within.
> I *am learning* to be confident and tall within.
> I *am becoming* confident and tall within.
>> I don't want to have low self-esteem
>> I am not afraid

To be sure:

- ◆ I am confident and tall within.

The peace of God in me ...

Sarah Dippity added as a side-bar, "Everyone has their own affirmations, desires and wishes. Each morning wake as well as each bed time my affirmation is this ..."

'The peace of God in me sees the peace of God in you...'

Chip away ...

For consummation
Chip away
Everyday
Upon waking ...
Before sleeping ...
And simply say ...
Your affirmation.

Big and bold ...

Garner your victory to be
response-able!!!
Write your affirmation
right here, right now!!!
Use

BIG ... **BOLD** ... **WORDS** ...

Step Five

CHOICE...

Quackers said, "Once you reach Step Five, you may have some energy to take action to latch on to your real self – *the confident you*. Or maybe you are recreating yourself."

Rigidity ...

Sarah Dippity cautioned, "If you show rigidity to Step Five move to Step One - Change Your Mind -- and move through each Step.

Angus chimed in, "Listing these Steps 1-7 implies sequence. Sequence is good yet you can move to whatever step fits you better. There is no set time to accomplish these steps. Consistency is the key. Everyone is different. The Steps are differently absorbed by each person.

Sometimes some Steps are stronger with you than other steps. You like one more than another. Do which one works for you, even if it's simply one Step, do that one then another, when you choose ... When you accomplish one of the Steps the next one seems easier. Also, the Steps are synergistic. Together they are more than the sum of their parts!"

Then Chris joined, "Maybe you are getting down on yourself -- that's OK. Your energy may be low. Step back from moving forward. Get down on yourself if you choose to - up to 20% of your time -- and then move on.

When you have enough energy you are ready to give yourself choices.

Choices are foundational to your life.

Choices are made with you or without you. You make the choice or someone else does. If you let it, life itself makes choices for you. Sometimes life gives you **turning points**. You know, those things in life that happen out of your control. None-the-less you make all the **choice points** after the turning point ..."

Very Empowering!!! ...

Paladin said, "Making your choices is very empowering. They will create your awesome attitude to get you through the day, through your challenges and, especially, through to you!"

CHOICE
IS POWERFUL.

Quackers said, "Making choices is a circular process described here line by line.

The more choices you create in your life,
the more control you have *of* your life;
the more control you have *of* your life,
the more self-power you have *within* your life;
the more self-power you have *within* your life,
the more choices you can create *in* your life!"

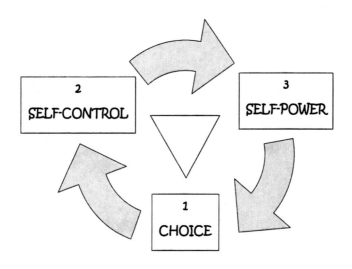

Blind to choice ...

It may not look like you have any choices right now. When it seems life hasn't given you any choices, it's easy to make excuses or rationalize your lack of choice.

However, **life always gives you choices**. You say there are no choices because you don't see them even though they are there.

Knowing yourself deeply is the bedrock of self-esteem.

This enables you to make more and more choices. Using these Steps progresses toward more self-esteem.

Knowing yourself deeply is the
bedrock of self-esteem ...

Feeling no worth or value blinds
you to see the choices. You have
to create a choice for yourself.

How do you make choices when
you don't see them?

Create ...

How do you create choice?

Ask yourself questions like – be pre-suppositional --

How can I make choices out of this situation?

Where can I be to get choices now?

What choices are out there, as yet, beyond my vision?"

Choices ...

One choice for you may simply be

- Do I want to take on this challenge the easy way or the hard way?

  Or

- Do I want to use this challenge for learning or for feeling sorry for myself?

  Or

- With this challenge will I have a great fall or will I find my balance and grow, and know myself more deeply?

IT'S ALL YOUR CHOICE!

Step Six

Energy...

Quackers ignited, "Energy is a measuring stick for life...

Energy is a useful unit to measure you and your life choices. Energy drives:

- ◆ your thoughts
- ◆ your emotions
- ◆ your actions

The drive ...

Energy is useful to use as an indifferent word and indicates no blame, no faults or excuses that may get you down, or put you into the 'blame game'. Energy can actually lift you up rather than put you down.

Use it in your daily language.

Objectify it ...

It's simply a unit...

You can objectify this part of life. It can drive your reasons for you to do some activity.

If you put energy out then how much energy do you get in return? If your out-energy is more than return-energy, perhaps you need to do something different.

Guilt-energy ...

If, for example, your guilt-energy is more than your return-energy then do something different. Rather than feel guilty-energy, change that to responsible-energy.

Take responsibility for what has triggered your guilt-energy.

Responsible-energy ...

If your guilt-energy comes out of
irresponsible action then rectify
it. Use your responsible-energy.
Honour the other person, learn
from it and do something different
the next time.

There is no room for guilt-energy
to live in responsible-energy."

There is no freedom without responsibility!!!!

Doing the right thing
Doing things right ...

If you did something responsible –
did things right – then move on.

There is no room for guilt-energy
to live in responsible-energy.

Energy ...

Energy can be objectified – it's simply a unit – a thing.

If you are feeling down and out, gathering low-energy, ask yourself,

'How long has this low-energy been pushing me around?'

'What can I do to change this low-energy into stimulating-energy?'

Draining ...

If you choose to avoid stimulating-energy, then stay where you are and use your feel-sorry-for-yourself- energy.

Feeling-sorry-for-yourself-energy takes energy away from you – VERY DRAINING!

There is NO return ...

... and worse ...

Zap ...

Unlike your value-energy that grows bigger the more you give away, feeling-sorry-for-yourself-energy **zaps** you exponentially.

You are invited to stay there if you choose to – up to 20% of your time. Then move on to Step 1."

Life is all about perspectives! When you notice things that appear less favourable in your life – realize this is *zapping* your enhanced-energy.

Focus ...

When you focus on what you perceive as unfavourable, these perspectives welcome more unfavourable things to enter your life. For example, if you buy a red car, now everyone seems to be driving a red car!

Unlike attracting unfavourable or favourable events - they are always there - it's how you see or perceive them. You make it one or the other. Maybe they are both!

Life is full of experiences and events. These are neither favourable nor unfavourable. It's how you decide to interpret them.

Gratitude-Attitude ...

Gratitude gives you attitude to focus on your perspectives that interpret events in an encouraging helpful way. Your gratitude magnifies your life-force energy! And this welcomes a more helpful perspective on life!!!!!

Step Seven

WHAT HAPPENS TO ALL
IS
THE GREAT FALL …

Quackers quoted a musical group. "'I get knocked down.

But I get up again.

They're never gonna keep me down.'" – *Chumbawamba - Tubthumping*

Down for the count ...

"Is life fair or unfair?

It's your choice.

You have been knocked down before and you will be knocked down again. This is life's program.

Getting knocked down is the first step in your growth. You may even get knocked down many times – and maybe you believe you get knocked down more than others."

Everyone's story has meaning for them no matter the size of the knock-down. So without minimizing you, Humpty, everyone gets knocked down. If you don't get knocked down, there is no growth.

That's life's program.

You get knocked down and tend to your hairline fractures. Tend to them to grow strong and affirmed.

It's easy to get knocked down; much harder to get back up."

Efficient ...

Quackers finished. "'Humpty Dumpty had a great fall

Humpty will get back up

Then Humpty will fall again

Humpty Dumpty may not be as up and down as a yo-yo but, none-the-less, has a fall ... gets back up ... has a fall ... gets back up ... has a fall ... gets back up ...'"

Seven steps ...

Yet, following the seven steps and paying attention to the hairline fractures, Humpty falls less, with less devastation and gets back up more efficiently and effectively!!!

Humpty Dumpty

GO FIGURED ...

... and so ...

... Humpty Dumpty lived
happily ever after!!!

The Beginning ...

The GO FIGURE Kids ...

With thanks to: E. Roger Muir, creator
and producer of Howdy Doody

American children's television...

What time is it kids,
ladies and gents?

It's ...

GO FIGURE TIME ...

Tell us what you did to make an unfavourable event turn into a valued event. How did you do that?
What will you be doing when you see life events work for you more often?

Tell us how you will be showing your gratitude-attitude?

...

CPSIA information can be obtained
at www.ICGtesting.com
Printed in the USA
LVOW07s0319011217
558271LV00002B/130/P